THE STATES AND THEIR SYMBOLS

Maryland
Facts and Symbols

by Muriel L. Dubois

Consultant:
Patricia Anderson
Editor
The Press at the Maryland Historical Society

Hilltop Books

an imprint of Capstone Press
Mankato, Minnesota

Hilltop Books are published by Capstone Press
151 Good Counsel Drive, P.O. Box 669, Mankato, Minnesota 56002
http://www.capstone-press.com

Library of Congress Cataloging-in-Publication Data
Dubois, Muriel L.
   Maryland facts and symbols/by Muriel L. Dubois.
   p. cm.—(The states and their symbols)
   Includes bibliographical references (p. 23) and index.
   Summary: Presents information about the state of Maryland, its nickname, motto,
and emblems.
   ISBN 0-7368-0523-0
   1. Emblems, State—Maryland—Juvenile literature. [1. Emblems, State—Maryland.
2. Maryland.] I. Title. II. Series.
CR203.M37 D83 2000
975.2—dc21   99-053463

Editorial Credits
Karen L. Daas, editor; Linda Clavel, production designer and illustrator;
   Kimberly Danger, photo researcher

Photo Credits
Bruce Coleman, Inc./Michael Ventura, 10; E. R. Degginger, 18
James P. Rowan, 16
One Mile Up, Inc., 8, 10 (inset)
Photo Agora, 6
Photo Network/Jim Schwabel, 22 (middle)
Rob and Ann Simpson, 12, 20
Unicorn Stock Photos/Ted Rose, 14; Mary Morina, 22 (bottom)
Visuals Unlimited/John D. Cunningham, cover; Bill Beatty, 22 (top)

1 2 3 4 5 6 05 04 03 02 01 00

Table of Contents

MARYLAND

Pennsylvania

West Virginia

Virginia

Fort McHenry
National Monument
and Historic Shrine

Baltimore ⬤ 🏛

🏛 National
Aquarium

Chesapeake Bay

Delaware

Washington, D.C. →

★ Annapolis

Assateague Island
National Seashore 🏛

Pacific Ocean

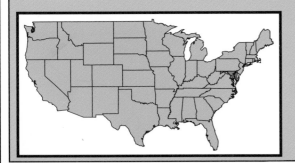

⭕	City
★	Capital
🏛	Places to Visit

Fast Facts

Capital: Annapolis is the capital of Maryland.

Largest City: Baltimore is Maryland's largest city. More than 645,600 people live there.

Size: Maryland covers 12,189 square miles (31,570 square kilometers). It is the 42nd largest state.

Location: Maryland is in the northeastern United States.

Population: 5,094,289 people live in Maryland. (U.S. Census Bureau, 1998 estimate).

Statehood: On April 28, 1788, Maryland became the 7th state to join the union.

Natural Resources: Miners dig coal from the ground in Maryland. Limestone, sand, and gravel are found in Maryland. The Chesapeake Bay has soft-shelled clams, oysters, and blue crabs.

Manufactured Goods: Factories in Maryland produce electrical equipment, steel, and computer software.

Crops: Farmers grow soybeans and corn. They also raise chickens for meat and eggs.

In 1632, King Charles I gave land in America to nobleman George Calvert. English settlers moved to the American colony. Calvert died before the charter for the land became official in 1634. Calvert's son, Cecil Calvert, planned the new colony. He named it Maryland after King Charles's wife, Queen Henrietta Maria.

Maryland has two nicknames. It is called the Old Line State and the Free State. Some people say General George Washington nicknamed Maryland the Old Line State. He wanted to honor the soldiers of Maryland who fought in the Revolutionary War (1775-1783).

The nickname the Free State came from Hamilton Owens. He was the editor of the *Baltimore Sun*. In 1923, Owens wrote articles in this newspaper that asked voters to think for themselves. He called Maryland the Free State when he wrote.

Maryland's nickname the Old Line State honors Revolutionary War soldiers. Today, people at Fort McHenry honor these soldiers by acting out battles.

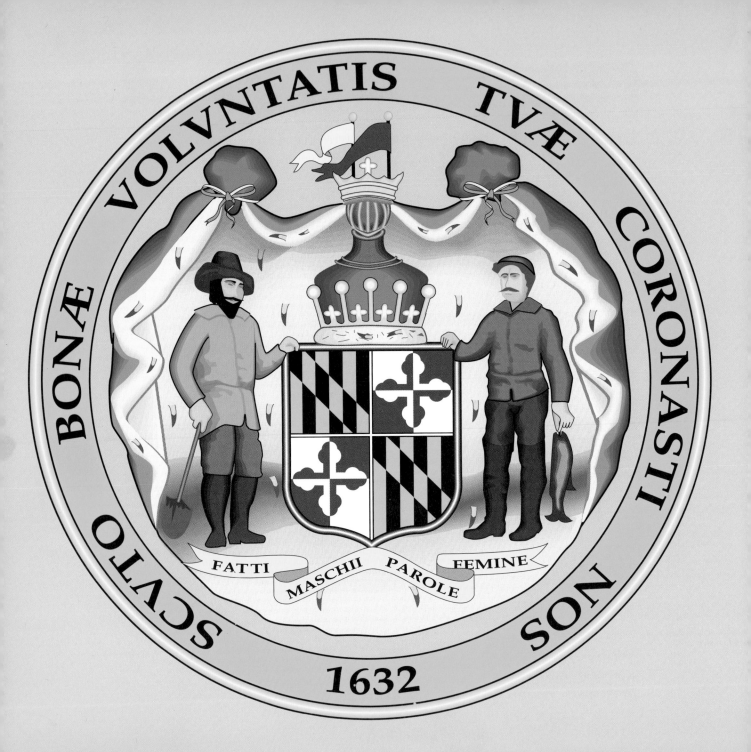

VOLVNTATIS TVÆ CORONASTI SCVTO BONÆ NOS

FATTI MASCHII PAROLE FEMINE

1632

State Seal and Motto

Maryland adopted its state seal in 1876. The seal reminds people of Maryland's state government. The seal also makes government papers official.

A shield is in the center of the seal. A farmer and a fisher hold the shield. The shield shows the coat of arms of two important families. The Calvert family coat of arms is yellow and black. The Mynne family coat of arms is red and white. George Calvert's mother was a Mynne.

Latin words appear on the border of the seal. They mean "With favor wilt thou compass us as with a shield." This means Maryland protects its people.

The state motto appears on a ribbon below the shield. The Latin motto means "Manly deeds, womanly words." The motto tells the people of Maryland to work hard, be strong, and use words to solve problems. The motto encourages people to use the strengths of both men and women.

The date 1632 appears on Maryland's seal. King Charles I gave George Calvert the charter for Maryland in 1632.

State Capitol and Flag

Annapolis is Maryland's capital city. The state capitol building is in Annapolis. Government officials meet in the capitol to make the state's laws.

Maryland's capitol is the oldest building still used by a state government. In 1772, workers completed the first section of the building. The building also served as the capitol of the United States from November 1783 to August 1784. During those months, the Continental Congress met there. The Continental Congress made laws for the United States.

Maryland's capitol has two domes. A small dome is on top of a larger one. The smaller dome holds a lightning rod. Inventor Benjamin Franklin designed the lightning rod.

The state flag has two crests on it. These crests also are on the state seal. The crests represent the Calvert and Mynne families.

Maryland's capitol building also is called the State House.

State Bird

In 1947, Maryland adopted the Baltimore oriole as its state bird. The bird's feathers are black and orange. The Baltimore oriole is named after the first Lord Baltimore. He often saw the bird at his estate in Maryland. Baltimore used the bird's colors as the colors for his shield.

The Baltimore oriole builds its nest with twigs, plants, and bark. The nest hangs from the tip of a tree branch. A Baltimore oriole lays about five eggs in the nest each year. The eggs are gray with brown or black spots.

The Baltimore oriole eats fruit and seeds. The bird also eats caterpillars, wasps, and insects. Every fall, the Baltimore oriole flies south. Orioles cannot find food during winter in the north.

In 1882, Maryland passed a law to protect its state bird. The Baltimore oriole was the first protected songbird in the United States.

Male Baltimore orioles have bright orange chests. Females have only small patches of orange.

State Tree

Maryland officials named the white oak as the state tree in 1941. The white oak also is called the Stave Oak. A stave is one of the slats of a wooden barrel. The white oak's wood was famous for making tight barrels that would not leak. Shipbuilders in Maryland also used wood from the white oak.

The white oak tree can grow to be 100 feet (30 meters) tall. The tree's broad, shiny leaves are green on the top and white on the bottom. They turn red in the fall. The white oak's seeds grow inside egg-shaped acorns.

The largest white oak tree in the United States grows in Maryland. The Wye Oak in Talbot County, Maryland, is more than 400 years old. This tree is 100 feet (30 meters) tall. In 1939, the state of Maryland purchased the Wye Oak and the area it grows on. Maryland made the land a state park. This was the first time a state bought a tree to preserve it.

White oak trees grow in fields throughout Maryland.

The black-eyed Susan is Maryland's state flower. A group of women chose the flower in 1896. The black-eyed Susan became the official state flower in 1918.

The black-eyed Susan shares the black and yellow colors of the Calvert coat of arms. The flower's petals are yellow and its center is black.

Black-eyed Susans need a lot of sun to grow. These wildflowers can grow up to 3 feet (90 centimeters) tall. Their leaves can grow to 6 inches (15 centimeters) long.

Black-eyed Susans bloom in late summer. Their flowers grow separately or in pairs. These flowers grow to be 2 inches (5 centimeters) to 6 inches (15 centimeters) wide.

Black-eyed Susans grow in all types of soil. They grow wild throughout Maryland and the eastern United States.

Black-eyed Susans are part of the daisy family of flowers. They also are called Sonoras daisies.

State Crustacean

In 1989, Maryland adopted the blue crab as the state crustacean. A crustacean is an animal with a hard shell. Crustaceans live mostly in the water. The blue crab is important to the state's economy. Crabtown is a common nickname for Annapolis.

Blue crabs have five pairs of legs. Their back legs are paddles. They allow blue crabs to swim. Male blue crabs have blue legs. Female blue crabs have blue legs with red-orange tips.

A female blue crab lays more than one million eggs at a time. She carries the eggs under her body and buries them on a sandy beach. The eggs hatch into larvas. These young blue crabs go through several more stages before they reach adulthood.

Crab is a popular food in Maryland. People prepare crab in many ways. They make crab cakes, crab dip, and crab soup. Crab cakes are served in many restaurants.

A blue crab grows a new claw if it loses one.

State Dog: In 1964, the Chesapeake Bay retriever became Maryland's state dog. This dog was one of the first breeds developed in the United States. Chesapeake Bay retrievers usually are brown and have light-colored eyes. People use these dogs to hunt birds.

State Fish: In 1965, Maryland adopted the striped bass, or rockfish, as its state fish. The striped bass can grow to be 6 feet (1.8 meters) long and weigh more than 100 pounds (45 kilograms).

State Insect: In 1973, the Baltimore checkerspot butterfly became the official state insect. The checkerspot butterfly's wings are black and yellow.

State Reptile: The diamondback terrapin became Maryland's state reptile in 1994. The diamondback terrapin was common in colonial times. By the late 1800s, the terrapin began to disappear. Laws now protect the turtle.

The diamondback terrapin lives in marshy areas near salt water.

Places to Visit

Assateague Island National Seashore

Assateague Island is in the Atlantic Ocean. The island is famous for its wild horses. They roam the 37-mile (60-kilometer) long island. Visitors to Assateague Island can visit horses, camp, or go canoeing. Visitors bike, swim, walk nature trails, and learn how to look for crabs.

Fort McHenry National Monument and Historic Shrine

Fort McHenry was built in 1798. Soldiers used the fort in every U.S. war until World War II (1939–1945). Francis Scott Key watched the bombing of the fort during the War of 1812 (1812–1815). The battle inspired him to write "The Star-Spangled Banner."

National Aquarium in Baltimore

The National Aquarium in Baltimore is seven stories tall. Its coral reef exhibit is in a tank that holds nearly 400,000 gallons (1,500,000 liters) of water. The aquarium is home to more than 10,000 marine animals. Visitors view sharks, dolphins, poison dart frogs, and many other animals.

Words to Know

charter (CHAR-tur)—an official, written document that gives a person or group the right to own a certain amount of land
coat of arms (KOHT UHV ARMZ)—a shield or a picture of a shield that has a design on it; the design is usually the symbol for a family, city, or state.
crustacean (kruhss-TAY-shuhn)—a sea animal with an outer skeleton; a crab is a crustacean.
economy (ee-KON-uh-mee)—the ways a city or state makes the money it needs
stave (STAYV)—one of the curved pieces of wood that forms the side of a barrel

Read More

Burgan, Michael. *Maryland.* America the Beautiful. New York: Children's Press, 1999.

Kummer, Patricia. *Maryland.* One Nation. Mankato, Minn.: Capstone Books, 1998.

Pietrzyk, Leslie. *Maryland.* Celebrate the States. New York: Benchmark Books, 2000.

Thompson, Kathleen. *Maryland.* Portrait of America. Austin, Texas: Raintree Steck-Vaughn, 1996.

Useful Addresses

Maryland Tourism Development Board
217 East Redwood Street
Baltimore, MD 21202

Office of the Secretary of State
Maryland State House
Annapolis, MD 21401

Internet Sites

50 States and Capitals
http://www.50states.com/maryland.htm
Kids' Page: Neat Stuff in Maryland
http://www.sos.state.md.us/sos/kids/html/kidhome.html
Stately Knowledge: Maryland
http://www.ipl.org/youth/stateknow/md1.html

Index